PRAISE FOR *THINGS A BRIGHT BOY CAN DO*

'Michael Chang's *Things a Bright Boy Can Do* continues their irreverent (although "irreverent" seems too quaint a word!) poetic project. Their serious hijinks include critiques of pop culture, politics, and the ugly excesses of the empire. A fourth-generation New York School poet, Chang is both frank—and Frank! O'Hara famously picked up *New World Writing* while Chang champions *Cobra Milk*. Chang's inventive poems take the shape of maps, bingo cards, lie detector tests, and a commencement address. The poems find themselves on LinkedIn, in chat rooms, with text abbreviations. Both comic and provoking, Chang is Fortune Feimster meets Sylvia Plath meets Gus Van Sant. They challenge the very nature of what a poem can do—and then sneak up on you with tender lines like "i sing to love singing" and "u loved me most in a poem." Chang's is a wild and wonderful original voice.'
— DENISE DUHAMEL, AUTHOR OF *BLOWOUT*

'Michael Chang's latest, *Things a Bright Boy Can Do*, is an electric, kaleidoscopic, queer, sexy, hilarious collection, a one-sided chat-room transcript, a chaotic house party where you're as likely to stumble across René Magritte as LeBron James, Kitty Dukakis, Foreigner, the Powerpuff Girls. Chang deftly backstrokes through the contradictions and ironies of our degraded age, their course bending always toward the persistence of desire, love. Chang writes, "high there r u still listening." We are. We can't help it. A wild, astonishing book.'
— EDGAR KUNZ, AUTHOR OF *FIXER*

'In an electrifying update on the spirit of the New York School, Chang takes us directly to the heart of the culture in these poems. As frantic and shifty as a TikTok stream, *Things a Bright Boy Can Do* is made of film clips, news items, heartbrokenness, poems O'Hara would have written if he'd had Tinder, and Chang swipes right on nearly everything. The voice is multiple, the forms are too, and the range of references is dizzying. I don't care how young or old you are, you will feel behind the eight ball watching these rapid-fire poems insert themselves into high, low, and every other culture at once. Sexual image intentional. And at the bottom of it all is a genuine love. You already have this book in your hands, so just walk up to the counter and buy it. It'll be fun.'

— MATTHEW ROHRER, AUTHOR OF *THE OTHERS*

'As Michael Chang writes in *Things a Bright Boy Can Do*, they agree: they are a great poet. Good. What a relief to meet a writer so completely unafraid of their own power, unaverse to danger, and ready for anything. This collection is another planet full of life in Chang's rapidly expanding universe, as rich in intellect and elegance as in comedic timing. Compare this work to nothing. Underestimate it and perish.'

— A. LIGHT ZACHARY, AUTHOR OF *MORE SURE*

'Michael Chang is back with their signature irrepressibility: the voice that bubbles with endlessly exuberant wit, encyclopedic pop culture references, playful orthography, and intense emotion. Are you here for poetry that can lure Superman, Dolly Parton, and Prince allusions together? Are you up for parataxis with a vengeance? If wordplay and irreverence are music to your ears, tune in to *Things a Bright Boy Can Do*.'

— EVIE SHOCKLEY, AUTHOR OF *SUDDENLY WE*

'Michael Chang's *Things a Bright Boy Can Do* pushes and pushes, and then pushes some more. It's provocative, fearless, and relentless, unafraid to reinvent tone, grammar, and just about everything else that dares to enter the path of Chang's perception. *Things a Bright Boy Can Do* is a ride on the back of a new modern language.'

— VICTORIA CHANG, AUTHOR OF *WITH MY BACK TO THE WORLD*

THINGS A BRIGHT BOY CAN DO

MICHAEL CHANG

COACH HOUSE BOOKS, TORONTO

copyright © Michael Chang, 2025

first edition

Published with the generous assistance of the Canada Council for the Arts and the Ontario Arts Council. Coach House Books also acknowledges the support of the Government of Canada through the Canada Book Fund

LIBRARY AND ARCHIVES CANADA CATALOGUING IN PUBLICATION

Title: Things a bright boy can do / poetry by Michael Chang.
Names: Chang, Michael (Poet), author.
Identifiers: Canadiana (print) 20250110245 | Canadiana (ebook) 20250114127 | ISBN 9781552454978 (softcover) | ISBN 9781770568495 (EPUB) | ISBN 9781770568617 (PDF)
Subjects: LCGFT: Poetry.
Classification: LCC PS8605.H35626 T45 2025 | DDC C811/.6—dc23

Things a Bright Boy Can Do is available as an ebook: ISBN 978 1 77056 849 5 (EPUB), 978 1 77056 861 7 (PDF)

Purchase of the print version of this book entitles you to a free digital copy. To claim your ebook of this title, please email sales@chbooks.com with proof of purchase. (Coach House Books reserves the right to terminate the free digital download offer at any time.)

TABLE OF CONTENTS

HOUDINI	9
TWENTY THOUSAND LEAGUES	11
OPPORTUNITY IS KNOCKING	13
FLOYD THE BARBER	15
ENFANT TERRIBLE	16
聊天室 CHAT ROOM	18
BAND OF OUTSIDERS	19
COMME DES GARÇONS	20
ILLUSTRATIONS THAT THE WORLD IS WHAT YOU MAKE IT	22
EVERYTHING IS PERFECT :)	24
IN THE NICK OF TIME	25
CROWN SHYNESS	27
POEM BEGINNING WITH LINE FROM MILLAY	29
'PER SAY'	30
少年诗人的心疤 SCARS OF A YOUNG POET	32
JACKIE DAYTONA	34
BABY DRIVE SOUTH	35
LINGUA IGNOTA	40
鬼地方 UNHOLY PLACE	42
低级趣味 DIRTY	44
LOOKOUT, LOOKOUT	45
MORE NIGHTS THAN DAYS	48
LOOK AT THE SUN	50
STICK TO MY SIDE	51
I LOVE YOU BUT I'VE CHOSEN DARKNESS	52
PINK SPELLS	54
HOW R U I HEAR SOHO IS A HELLSCAPE NOW	55
HETEROSEXUALITY	56
SEXY VILLAIN	57

SHRINKWRAPPED	58
DEVIANT MESSIAH	59
ATONEMENT	61
SOLO SLUMBER PARTY	62
ORIENTAL CENTO WITH LINES FROM O'HARA	63
EPHRATA, PENNSYLVANIA	64
HUSBANDS DO NOT BE ALARMED	65
ORIENTAL POEM BINGO	66
DRINK BEFORE THE WAR	67
挪威森林 NORWEGIAN WOOD	68
DINNER PARTY	69
PENGUIN BEACH	71
原来你是这种人 SO THAT'S HOW U R	73
TAKE ME BACK INTO THE TWILIGHT	74
ANOTHER DREAMLESS NIGHT	75
NATE GROWING UP	76
JOCKSTRAP	77
HERE WE GO FOREVER	78
HAPPY POEM FOR HAPPY PPL	79
MISSISSIPPI	81
LIE DETECTOR	82
DON'T LET ME SPEND THE NITE WITH TEARS	84
BREAKING EVERY RULE FOR ME	86
I CHECKED UR CELLPHONE	87
MANDELA EFFECT	88
KING OF THE WORLD	89
COWLICKS	90
SAINT DES SAINTS	92
CIRCUIT CITY IS BURNING	94
COMMENCEMENT ADDRESS	95
MY SAD CAPTAINS	97

SAN ANTONIO	98
SWALLOW YOUR POISON	99
慢走不送 C U NEXT TUESDAY	101
WORLD'S LAST RECORD STORE	102
FUZZY DICE	103
FIRST WE KILL ALL THE ROLY-POLIES	104
BING CHILLING	106
ELEPHANT CASTLE	107
RETURN TO SENDER	109
GENEALOGY	110
MOMOFUKU	111
PRETTY BOY EW	112
PRIVATE / PUBLIC	113
ANGEL'S SHARE	114
MOTHER OF MUSES	115
WE'RE ONLY MOUTH	116
DO I REALLY HAVE NOTHING AT ALL	117
MOLLY RINGWALD / PORTRAIT OF A LADY	118
SECONDHAND GOD	119
READY FOR THE ECSTASY	120
ALL THE HUSKIES ARE EATEN	122
FORMER MUSE	123
IT'S NOT A SAD THING	124
COPY & PASTE	125
THINGS A BRIGHT BOY CAN DO	126
SOME FREE ADVICE	127
AREN'T YOU SUNSET?	128
ACKNOWLEDGEMENTS	131
ABOUT THE AUTHOR	133

HOUDINI

pence referring to trump as his 'former running mate'
is like nick cannon calling mariah one of his exes

the man whose head screwed on sideways
real fit / somebody else's heirlooms

the revised wedding vows over there
a sleazy sort of enchantment

ocean of mirror balls & velvet jumpsuits
it is in some respects abt homos

i believe it was the homo who said he was incapable of cutting down
but stopping would actually be possible [how reductive]

hide a penny under his tongue
make the taste more palatable

nipples glistening raison d'être [go figure]
u ain't fuck me u fuck the old body

golden raisins that's no longer me
time turns into a fiction

believing these stories abt god
slumming it at the hay-adams

that's how u know i'm a native [that hyphen]
a good listener

alice claims i sing to love singing
i caught u murmuring just to say something

well i seem to have misplaced my charger
don't know much but the name ain't alice,
nancy

TWENTY THOUSAND LEAGUES

to get on my level
most will need a ladder
stretching thru forever

waiting on ur stoop
the spanish steps
we were touch & go
for a while there

this label-required ballad
turned our eyes into searchlights
trained on some blond fantasy
u pulled on like taffy

yes
hitting it exactly
surviving on coffees movies & teevee
lured into kissing frogs for renminbi

bellyful of garlic sausage & baked beans
the dancers gassy but happy
incidentally
chinatown is ur favourite movie

u will have to excuse this glut of new work
i find myself incredibly inspirational
yet far away mentally
—the warm imagery of u

thumbs hooked into pockets
adorned w. shiny rivets

(soon) a wordless routine
—dirt soaped off
suds clogging drains
ur bed no place for a lady

pâté offal & aspic will not elude
beth ditto's gossip
go on
eat the croissant
tempt fate while ur at it
i've kept u well-fed knowing
there are
in this life
no unceasing banquets

OPPORTUNITY IS KNOCKING

in a blaze of consciousness

the authorities put the ski instructor to death

the difference between a croque madame & a croque monsieur

being an egg

but u don't need egg, u need boyfriend

monster too tame

to capture whales in vain

or brush w. elongated device the hippo's teeth

melissa mccarthy grunting & wanting bourbon

defusing bomb w. cuticle scissors

as meredith vieira berates her for pace & posture

figuring out LLC formation & the best pipe

amidst mare's nest of united global services pax

faceless w. monogrammed luggage sets

we conduct ourselves honourably

i scan ur nipples w. my thumbs

maybe rewatch *days of being wild* w. these doritos ranch

bear w. me & perhaps u already know this

but ppl don't tell the truth or keep their promises

—i do

i just want a perfect day w. u

then another & another & another & another

till i have endless perfect days w. u

right now

FLOYD THE BARBER

it begins — blades so precarious — they quiver w. dew — the bull w.
gleaming eyes — mounts a huge horsefly — hard as spurs — but that
was before — young toreros cast long shadows — as for me — the
oars to ur boat — i'm in the water — ur in the wind — demeanour
loose as sails — why did u decide — one way or another — to be awful

ENFANT TERRIBLE

everything i do is for the sixteen-year-old me / maybe

boy refusing to take off the kenzo dress / thx for ur unflinching honesty

thirty-seven years ago / on this day / five teens had saturday morning detention

my mantra / squeaky wheel gets the grease / nobody ghost me but casper

life comes in many flavours / death / drug use / racism / sex / shaming / violence / combat

& ppl doing their best !!! / introducing powerpoint to the french

writing those poems w. numbered sections / all boring

engaging in intense / ambiguously romantic relationships

haunting the rest of their lives / uncertain but hopeful

human wrecks / so lost & wounded / hurting those closest to them

gallantly making art / longing & rage compressed into single lines uniformed boys to the front / pig me / find ur happiness

we're animals more equal than others / tugging ourselves w- passionate self-love

i retch at the sight of foie gras / iz so good

i'm not interested in dying / by which i mean talking abt the act of dying

go write abt the hoarfrost / muse over fkn rivers / why don't u

the king of hearts had five sons / 超级偶像 / well dam iz me

tricks / secrets / illusions & reveals / i suffer / kind of admiringly

keep cum & carry on / à la charli's white mercedes / frank's white ferrari

before i loved u / i prepared myself to write bad cheques / readied myself to waver

such is our grown-up love song / many reflections / countless destinies

this bizness / iz abt timing / if i came back / would u hold it against me ???

聊天室 CHAT ROOM

Murmur ur secret desires !

        ur hapless & emotional notes on love !

                ur naked struggling !

At last I've realized wut others have perhaps !

        been saying all along !

Which is ur emotional unavailability !

      & FEAR of intimacy !

           & FEAR FEAR FEAR !

& that u DO like me !

     that is the problem !

       I have u & u have me !

Depraved heart !

     is this wut is meant by 'a good problem to have' !

BAND OF OUTSIDERS

The Empress is kind ; like Yoko Ono ; sent to a farm upstate ; my trauma stems from being too excellent ; I wrote abt Lukas Gage getting rimmed & then he came out ; I believe that is causation / wish fulfillment ; an instance being the jacket crimson with use ; rich & lush & tinged with exactly the kind of Americana that made Ralph Lauren (born one Ralph Lifshitz) a global star ; capable of guiding its wearer thru any ensuing adversity / struggle with an almost mythical quality ; the KMT patches & slight crop suggesting its wearer ready to tackle challenges in this new era ; its borderline effeminacy promising new perspectives (!) without sacrificing hot-blooded principle ; to vanquish enemies in style ; buy COBRA MILK™ !!! ; available at most major retailers ; forty-eight contiguous states & D.C. only ; other restrictions may apply

COMME DES GARÇONS

here's what's happened since u were last on linkedin

ur dirty sayonara

this lifestyle yanked away from me

ludwig kim jones fav boi he put his fats on it

o'hara considering the muse as demon lover

plath looking into the eyes of demon lover

this jack of hearts

always drinking too much

in the middle of a kiss

florida man

wasted like confetti

b mine

please confirm

i'm hooked in a bad way

we'll put osiris on the case

don't eat stuff off the sidewalk

i promise u come first

like a lover like a song

it starts & ends w/ u

don't b afraid if nobody loves u

i've been trying to tell u

one day at a time

ILLUSTRATIONS THAT THE WORLD IS WHAT YOU MAKE OF IT

1: a potter's fingers; nimble; especially the thumb

2: grand sweep & details exactly the same; macrocosm & microcosm identical

3: prologues to what's possible

4: restatement of romance; ur a service to mankind; i wasn't aware my membership had lapsed

5: dream of immense sadness; help!

6: international iq test—start the test

7: men, you'll never need the blue pill again; try this tonight!

8: fighting diabetes? this discovery leaves doctors speechless!

9: forget the blue pill; just take this once daily

10: 7 mysterious photos that can't be explained

11: 10 strange animals you probably didn't know exist

12: black champion edition mesh jumbo t-shirt; $227 ~~$360~~

13: three-pack grey champion edition jersey briefs; $189 ~~$370~~

14: pointlessly handsome; spread-eagled in the schoolyard; udders splayed richly across my face

15: the great detective; sherlock holmes; so close i could see the whites of his knuckles

16: i kiss ur cup; i know so much

17: epic song; one for the ages

18: we do *not* publish poetry!!!

EVERYTHING IS PERFECT :)

glowering roughnecks pining for angels until sick love a fussy sort of discipline these feelings like blasts of ice they say meet me where hooters used to be i trawl thru change dot org b/c i want to know wut futility feels like a childless milf a5 wagyu whiteboys so insane for pleasure they forget themselves we hear the stars grinding to dust 'i bought u a sweater u don't have it yet i hope ur not too cold' ur mascara's running & that's my dick ur eyes gleaming w/ wet dreams mirrors might steal ur charm u lower ur swollen membranes 靠你不如靠北 not all muses are created equal i have unqualified admiration for u u impress me so much ur mallorca wedding u invited the jennifer lawrence his destiny is to be w/ me omg wut if he forgotten me like chris brown forgotten ur right it's impossible juicy nubs fail us he is my only metric

IN THE NICK OF TIME

1

I find the worst of all possible boys:

wet-cheeked, slack-jawed & big-tongued

(The duck puts down his coat) (The lake freezes over)

A heart-shaped void

2

Yearning for the soft caress of oppression

I'm a whore for brutality

It's all fear

It seems gentle now

3

Thank God

A sigh of relief

I set myself free

We are orphans

4

We'll always have New York, I write but don't mean

Don't call last min

Erase me

Leave only the alphabets

CROWN SHYNESS

Am quite confident in my knowledge of geography until pressed to differentiate between Bucharest & Budapest ... know next to nothing abt Vladivostok

So funny how the *Paris Review* can correct their use of Jan Morris's pronouns (good) but utterly fail to contextualize her abhorrent views on empire. Consider this gem abt the British Empire ... 'There was a general rule of fair play abt it'

I see that elegance is a struggle for u ... have u tried restarting ur computer ???

Pls stop writing abt how ur cells supposedly turn over every seven years & u become a different person

Life is just a series of meaningless melancholies ... a picnic w/ ghastly food

Frustrated desires in Magritte's enshrouded faces ... a frog upside down ... belly exposed

Handsome like a ghost ship ... squeaky like a phantom doll ... u drink DayQuil hoping to fall asleep

Yes tell us abt ur MOON POEM ... cold silvery love-pity & sperms (!)

My take on the 'foreign words' thing is we should randomly italicize Anglo words like ~wharf~

SEA SURFACE FULL OF CLOUDS ... stray comment from Oprah leading to minor boating accident

The radicals meet in any one of a million Think Coffees where no actual thinking occurs

I resent these small indignities … ur tacky champagne Rolls-Royce w/ the coach doors

Was it my subtle / quick intellect or the broad spread of my ass / love canal ???

He loves me b/c my pores secrete fragrance … wut my body makes ppl adore … I like his flashy looks

Whereas … be it resolved … fill me w/ white light & strangers who kiss

Under a red hat … a boy-face made of words

The disgraced moving company KANE IS ABLE

Stolen valour … sad splendour of battered gold

Birds refusing to rebuild old nests

Érase una vez … pero ya no

I would give u my life (but I'm using it) (granted I'll never be the same w/o u)

POEM BEGINNING WITH LINE FROM MILLAY

i will be the gladdest thing under the sun!

headfirst in yummy stank   gnawing like a mouse

modest yet menacing   this two-seater benz   doomsday express

velvet-rope veteran   peddling irresponsible love

not ur god but lick u top-to-bottom   do such a good job

employee of the month

keep me in ur pocket doraemon   steady relationship   ???

[no record found]

takes talent to be a dick   yea   bravo

sweet pink skies   how did we go sideways

loved us in pink   background noise as ambient music

31 flavours   98 degrees   kevin bacon   we were never close

u character actor   stroke as ur method

my favourite person in the whole wide world

day two   key to the city   i could've loved u more   in the dark

happy as fuck but still lonely   peak of my powers   ???

u wouldn't know everest even if it climbed u

'PER SAY'

timid as a houseplant , horny watching *avatar* ,

someone seeing u , knowing u so intimately , can be a terrifying thing ,

u hiss , savage blossom ,

stupid , weak , what a waste

●

u want a drip but i'm a tsunami , of feeling , per say ,

my george miles , a bad imitation , i'm never sure & ur never right ,

call off ur goons , cycle of violence & that ,

which unsavoury personage hurt u

●

clay pigeon , bird's-eye view ,

ur allegiance to something that maybe never was ,

robot crime family , no half-measures ,

something abt bivalves , something abt a heart

●

light on ur breath ,

take a dip ,

river ,

suck a shrimp head

●

for those who burn in the memory of love ,

the gentleman will suspend ,

the gentleman will suspend ,

as if already dead

少年诗人的心疤 SCARS OF A YOUNG POET

three books in a year . more on the way . all my poems diss tracks

ur faux friends jealous u have me

they prob order avo toast & watch bill maher

try to bring u down . crabs in a bucket

we won't see them at the players . the drinks defcon 1

i don't mean to be squeamish . i know ur strong . independent . like omarosa

confident in milano . tongue-tied in paris . flights always cleared to land

don't mind the silver spoon . tell u what i think

most ppl obsessed w/ youth . for the possibilities

like reading playboy . for the articles

dark mouth of a park . crypto traders in weehawken

we eat doughnuts . play xbox . listen to justice pam sneed

i accept ur cud . expectantly . u talk abt my queer wiles . by which u mean my love for u

we go together lime & cola . my only daddy issues when daddy don't listen . nonononono

wanna lie w/ u . hop on it . defy gravity chicagoland speedway

i was urged . couldn't say no . couldn't tell victory from anguish

ur eyes flashing . u want a thaw . a release . timeless slipstream of maker & muse

u can underline it . put it on a t-shirt . i won't let u suffer alone

my apple computer . so grateful for life

JACKIE DAYTONA

wut cracked shutters

wut idle bottles

wut shuffling feet

the goldenest inhabitant, face impassive like a centurion's

flush w/ machismo & feigned indifference

my OG muse, plucked from obscurity, concerned only w/ secret things

easily missed in the heart of pines

that the unforgiving cold, a marital bed, should speak to him

eyes coaxing, language exacting

page after page

a blueblood

fat & guzzly

a humble scribe

humbly served

BABY DRIVE SOUTH

Cole SWENSEN choked on a gummy worm

Monica YOUN worked sixteen-hour days at the circus

D. A. POWELL denied his involvement in Medicare fraud

Forrest GANDER caused his publisher to shutter after
eighty-four years in business

Mary RUEFLE was revealed to be the actor Danny Glover on shrooms

Kay RYAN impersonated Childish Gambino to enter
Justice Sotomayor's chambers

Marianne MOORE once dated the singer Sade

Natalie DIAZ was Diana's one true love

Gerald STERN was arrested for butchering the rules of Connect Four

Henri COLE graduated first in his class at the police academy

Ken CHEN died of sadness

Dan BEACHY-QUICK caused the building to collapse

Robert HASS insisted on calling himself 'rudeboy'

Rae ARMANTROUT called America a third-world country while
running for U.S. Senate

Ada LIMÓN was breathy on the subway

Dorianne LAUX accosted a man for birdwatching

Marilyn CHIN laced her mooncakes with arsenic

Don Mee CHOI pretended to be twelve years old

Dan CHIASSON witnessed a crime against humanity

Robert CREELEY claimed he was related to the new commissioner
to secure a promotion

Jorie GRAHAM got into a shouting match over Ina Garten's
pineapple upside-down cake

Jericho BROWN was sued for defamation in the State of New Jersey

Sharon OLDS was the young W. S. Merwin

Dean YOUNG had an angry cold sore

Ocean VUONG giggled 'light skin' to refer to his egg roll

John WIENERS called Jack Spicer a fugly slut

John BERRYMAN had to be duct-taped to his seat

Tyehimba JESS googled himself but didn't care for the results

Charles BERNSTEIN beat out my friend for a teaching job

Vijay SESHADRI gave us a tour of his extensive gardens

Gregory PARDLO waited so long he turned to stone

Theresa Hak Kyung CHA outlived her murderer

Tracy K. SMITH criticized the president's rug &
was never heard from again

Matthew DICKMAN was so upset he could not stand

Michael DICKMAN was investigated by another agency due to
a conflict of interest

Paul MULDOON told you his horse was larger than yours

CACONRAD sent anthrax to Betsy DeVos & was awarded
the Medal of Freedom

Elaine EQUI gaslit the waitress who confused her with Anita Hill

Natasha TRETHEWEY ordered a Denver omelette well done

Lyn HEJINIAN beat the lie detector with time-tested KGB tactics

Jean VALENTINE misused PPP funds to expand her bonsai collection

Adrienne RICH won the ugly-sweater contest every year

Robert PINSKY was found in the trunk of a 2004 Honda Civic

Randall MANN was appointed the next Transportation Secretary

Alice NOTLEY rode a soft wolf for different distances

Brenda HILLMAN invented a language so no one would speak to her

James TATE said his favourite word was 'tetas'

Campbell MCGRATH was buried with Old Bay Seasoning

Patricia SMITH taught me how to use chopsticks

Donald HALL had a wide stance at the Minneapolis airport

Charles SIMIC claimed that the Democrats have abandoned
'Middle America'

Don SHARE was the tea girl at *Interview*

Kaveh AKBAR was a palindrome

Franz WRIGHT was supposed to pick out new curtains
but hated everything

Adrian MATEJKA was gone when you woke up

Frank BIDART needed rehydration in a hurry

Kazim ALI was recuperating at home when the anal bead
lodged in his throat

Diane SEUSS saw that ass shaking

Mark DOTY said fake love don't last

Arthur SZE wanted to see the manager immediately

A. E. STALLINGS broke a priceless artifact & compensated
by working as a docent

Deborah LANDAU told Elizabeth Olsen she was excellent in *Mother*

Kim ADDONIZIO met her match in Courtney Love & surrendered

Wanda COLEMAN called your book 'second-rate'

June JORDAN said she hadn't read it

Rita DOVE picked up her glass & looked around skeptically

Ellen Bryant VOIGT opined loudly on 'the colonies'

Matthew ZAPRUDER secretly acquired Russian citizenship

Matthew ROHRER was announced as the newest judge
on *America's Got Talent*

Thomas LUX appeared on *The Voice* but was quickly eliminated

J. D. MCCLATCHY excused himself & devoured the hors d'oeuvres

Mary OLIVER was incapacitated by a rare disease
imported by Angelina Jolie

Wayne KOESTENBAUM was airlifted to the
Children's Hospital of Philadelphia

Carolyn FORCHÉ didn't want to go too fast

John ASHBERY was not available for comment

LINGUA IGNOTA

as mclaren famously said … there's no finish line …

u can always improve, iterate, evolve

an enormous appetite … the promise of a threat

dip it in u like gouache … art begins here

ppl regurgitating the same tired advice abt reading

& world-building & 'arcs' ad nauseam

i just write snarky feel-good shit !!!

i don't care abt ur arcs, wanna study ur curves

maybe andy cohen can tell me why colin firth & nick hoult

don't F in *a single man*, is he not over bridget

when i go onto the internet to engage u

i'm fishing for summery romantic icons

christopher atkins in *blue lagoon*

william hurt in *body heat*

drenched in colour, a strong yellow

sun-kissed portofino

any number can win

ur naked ankles

fetishized like jaden's pregnant dragons

roar of unbearable solleone

room for everyone in poetry & in bed

bees in the spell of a queen

ur nightmares are her business

the sweetest bois cause the nastiest breakups

u loved me most in a poem

鬼地方 UNHOLY PLACE

u try so hard for everyone else, wut abt doing something for urself

google search: charlie puth height

brodsky claimed that birds in poems = the poet themselves

more likely: birds in poems = carl phillips

i'd rather get squished by a tank than write abt tiananmen

shush, sanctimonious cathy

change the label, still sewage in a bottle

i'm a serious child, ur an ekphrastic of an ekphrastic

when i was a preteen & closer to death

i was ashamed for the boy & his bike

huge, shiny & new

so practised at lifting my legs, separating from reality

shaft me, gig economy

i rely on a strength, it comes from inside

i wait to walk behind u, stare gratuitously

u have the same idea, so clever

i look twice

there is dignity in work

piss hitting the back of a statue

soon ur breathing on me

elevator in limbo: sixteenth floor

knowing how to proceed: another kind of surrender

低级趣味 DIRTY

'fugly poetry cover' — — arguably its own aesthetic

ur eye on so many unmentionables — — they call u reconnaissance man

ur mind raging — — u want a piece

rejecting my call — — a roach move

in the days ppl cared more abt matchbox twenty

i did nothing — — i got lucky

lazy chinese — — won't play to type

tres — — pass

turn — — around

we hope u enjoyed the free articles

LOOKOUT, LOOKOUT

THERE ARE POWERFUL PPL BEHAVING BADLY & THEN
THERE'S ED BUCK

Ed Buck, California Democratic Donor, Is Convicted In 2 Deaths

Ed Buck Convicted In Meth Overdose Deaths Of Two Black Men

*Democratic Donor Ed Buck Is Convicted In Deaths Of 2 Men He Offered
Drugs For Sex*

Democratic Megadonor Ed Buck Guilty In Party-n-Play Drug Deaths

*White Gay Men Are Destroying Queer Black Lives With Party 'n' Play
Sex & Meth Addiction*

So what ur essentially saying is this man was a serial killer who
operated in plain sight in WeHo, not only known to law enforce-
ment but celebrated & fêted by the highest-ranking law enforce-
ment officials in the jurisdiction

What's interesting abt this case is that the prosecutor-in-charge
was a Black woman, a Democrat in an overwhelmingly Democratic
area & she did nothing

She was terrible ... a fascinating thing I noticed when I volunteered
for the now-DA's campaign is that many of his volunteers were in
fact attorneys in our office. She was so hated by line prosecutors
outside of her immediate circle that her employees were actively
working to defeat her

Don't forget the Sheriff's Office, which is its own nightmare ... there are outright gangs operating out of that office ... thugs with badges ... there was of course the infamous internal email list of 'acceptable' (like-minded, loyal) employees & members of white supremacist cliques ... that list was used to determine assignments, promotions & so on, it mattered more than anything else, it was dispositive

'That the facts have been brought to light means the system is working' ...

Ppl don't know how to react to this case b/c a powerful person was seemingly held to account for his horrific actions. It happens so rarely that collectively we don't quite know how to react

Do we really think that Ed Buck's donations alone held off law enforcement for that long? I think, as we've seen with Epstein & Weinstein, it's usually some combination of money, favours & straight-up blackmail

Maybe this is, as Obama says, a teachable moment & the powers-that-be will use this opportunity to examine the policies & procedures that led us to this awful place ... like what processes allowed these crimes to go unabated for so long? But I doubt it, ppl will cheer the verdict & then they will move on with their lives

Do we think the identity of those murdered mattered more than the demographics or party affiliation of the murderer? Black, gay, unhoused, battling addiction, turning to sex work/PNP ...

There's definitely that fetishization thing. POC being the sexual playthings of often rich, usually white, men

Yea, it's the 'cost of doing business' ... ur ticket to ride ... it just so happens that POC always get the short end of the stick

Especially in Hollywood, where there's been a level of acceptance relating to the casting couch, trading sexual favours for jobs ... it's like ok producers are creeps & politicians are crooks, it's rare to find cases that actually breach ppl's moral & ethical red lines

A predator's a predator. Party has nothing to do with it. It shouldn't be used as a political cudgel

He should've gotten more years like the Durst fella

Yea, definitely

MORE NIGHTS THAN DAYS

As a husband & daughter, I care abt this social justice issue & only b/c I am a husband & daughter

*

There are literally no other reasons I would concern myself w/ such issues as poverty, hunger ... desire encroaching upon me, rude like asking Adele who did her lap-band

*

Baked potatoes, bubbly, caviar, crème fraîche, maybe a truffle to kick it up a notch ... the magnitude of my obsessions will shock / impress (???) u

*

U BUILD BACK BETTER, have a whites-only bar thx to Biden ... he can't remember his lines but he'll never forget Scranton

*

His poems are weak b/c he doesn't dive deep ... he also hates himself, is incapable of separating love from jealousy

*

When u open ur eyes they submit to u ... elbow one another to become ur conquests tingly w/ use ... when u close ur eyes they dissipate ... kinda delighted, u say I seem to have come out of nowhere

*

Ur distant but not quite unattainable ... still legible, like inscriptions meant for somebody else ... forcibly I reorder my memories, shape

them to bypass u ... flick from thought to thought, unrecognizable,
rendered such that I associate them w/ anything other than u

*

I service young u & u don't want ppl to know ... u become something
I carry, an animal shivering in death ... the deer u once shot & wrote
abt, pistons pumping just fast enough to hang on

*

They aren't kidding ... u are otherworldly

LOOK AT THE SUN

precocious as a palanquin [+] sharply dressed [+] easily bored

drinking dom like beer [+] hustling like a youth

my face a genius grant [+] england is my city

ataxically

break it down gayle

iz not even close venus

how is lil bug-eyed luca

don't care abt loss [+] get outta my sight

i want daffodils [+] dandelions [+] an easy summer

bust my iron dome [+] reams [+] reams [+] no ulterior motives

MGK [+] his malcontents [+] fucks for every budget

something in ur throat [+] catarrh [+] the lying-down kind

vague green mist [+] pyramids panting

hu jintao on his wedding nite

collapsing

naomi i choose tom holland [+] final answer [+] locked in!

everything subject to change! (((((a boomerang!

i once told someone i would do anything for them

it wasn't a lie

but u knew that

STICK TO MY SIDE

i'm the pus ur the wound]
set me loose on ur lovely brim i do i do]
in my faithful mouth rummaging seeeeed]
so much floods ur chaotic discharge]
the intelligence services deem u an imbecilic threat]
handle ur bizness go abt ur day]
hide crusty undies]
take weedwacker to shin]
obedience such an awesome idea]
gimme dat coin tell us when u were born]
we never have to see dat day again]
scary words is it concrete or in my head]
don't be ridiculous we don't do poetry here]
maybe i've spent too much time apologizing]
i mean]
for u]

I LOVE YOU BUT I'VE CHOSEN DARKNESS

the loneliest boy in the world

secure in his position

the only girl in the world

quoting frank bidart

both me

i'm talking abt me

wanting white bees & grasshoppers lascivious

fried ant toast & buzzing insects in tea

{LEVELS OF A FOOD POEM:

1. Look at this disgusting food
2. I eat spoil
3. U will eat our ~exotic~ food & u will praise it}

don't forget tiny crickets & drunken noodle

how's that for meta ???

deliverance meet my jiffy lube

we get on like houses on fire

wonderful joyous streaks of orange

we skedaddle, twiddling w/ this manuscript

i knock & announce

i'd rather be by myself

{a torn veil

loving in secret

PINK SPELLS

brilliant boy-poet, like u hand-to-mouth

hair gushing from pits, can't say i appreciate it

strange smells, comme ci, comme ça

M & B go motorboating

a look of intent, deep as life

'sea monkeys' vaguely racist

in awe of cobblestones & carabinieri

the ones who dress sharp but can't fight

them balls, no one bats a thousand

imagine, we understand it too well

divagation & being a diva

some things only a bright boy can do

hey has that ever happened to u

high there r u still listening

HOW R U I HEAR SOHO IS A HELLSCAPE NOW

		test		save	an	a	
disgusting	undo	ur	a	the	image	particular	how
radiance	ur	fertility	form	good	u	slant	do
	top	on	of	stuff	planned		you
	button	my	erasure	for	on	divine	plead
		chin		me	introducing	intervention	

HETEROSEXUALITY

Should I wait for you in the car?

↕

I'll wait for you outside

SEXY VILLAIN

Everywhere I go in this city all I hear are white womyn sighing u are
so boring he had to be blind-drunk he was sloshed honey beer beer
beer saké after saké how is Snowden's sojourn

Enjoy the poetry better if u know nothing abt me DMs open show
me ur FRIDGE kicked to the 'kerb' I have never ventured to Park of
Ozone clam sauce order up

Gordon Ramsay says cheese & fish don't go together I force-feed him
tuna casserole till he stops yelling how do I get u alone

I lie when I say the ghost emoji is my favourite copying Marc Jacobs
the red balloon is actually my favourite

Brooklyn Beckham invites me to masturbate I'm so enamoured w/
his bedhead farmer's tan that I only touch him w/ tongue like delicate
flower he comes rather quickly cum lingers on his sausage fingers fat
w/ manly the livestream keeps going the comments unrelenting

Don't mean to lack decorum disturbed by description of David Wojna-
rowicz 'writing like a bottom' wonder who's the better basketball
player LeBron or Michael Jackson possibly

Extremely feverishly into Lee Ann Roripaugh's portrayal of lifeguards
as 'lovesick grapes' I want to be bowl to contain greedy u already
know they are bruised like wine it sux when pretty ppl disappoint I
just don't have it in me to wash the fucking dishes

SHRINKWRAPPED

marked from birth // armed w. nothing but a fertile imagination // & aggressively siphoned client records // the clearest implication being // i can read & shave my legs at the same time // in fairness it's exhausting being this talented // we can all sleep under phoebe bridgers // confusing kohl for monkey's wager // fresh evidence suggesting rejected pokémon // cast morgan freeman as god // to raise a glass for pete davidson's jewish charity // u left one brisk evening // off-limits as teenaged thighs // in which case we shouldn't be talking // using the first-person singular // promise u won't give away the plot // the pilfering foxes must come inside // pee everywhere // tear my house apart // still, it hurts

DEVIANT MESSIAH

POEM DESCRIBING REDDIT DEBATE BETWEEN 'COULD CARE LESS' & 'COULDN'T CARE LESS'

Total Immersion Poetry Workshop 2022

It is said that Paddington Bear, honeyed creature ostensibly from England, is from 'darkest Peru'

I never thought I'd grow up to be the person who wore shorts—albeit v cute—to a gallery opening

This reminds me of the time *GQ* featured my friends but cut me out b/c I was in shorts

In some poems, the looking-away, the not yet! not now!, the first-let-me! can be appealing

I have a bracket of boys who luv me & of coz u come out on top

When the hungry mouth is prest / I feel v blest

I gift u purple fluff, remake ur whole body

Ur belly button smells like tea-smoked duck

Arguments of counsel are not evidence

I emerge from my bedroom dramatically tho I live alone for the moment—wut u into

Never doubt American ingenuity, given the many varieties of pretzel

The shampoo is 'UNISEX' … u seem v animated over this

Insecure mxn luv to test how much u care & sometimes they go overboard … 我尽力了

U were so irate u took fingernails left in a library book, cloned the DNA, scolded the clone for hours, then married it

I jinxed it when I called u my Larry Rivers, didn't I

Such a funny word, 'lunchpail' ... almost excuses the slop

I do not need to know the origins of the word 'crabcake'

I'm so original I still use tokens on the subway

As Sontag (I know) said in 2000: 'Authority, idiosyncrasy, velvet-iness—these are what make a star'

U say there are no standards but they are talking abt me nevertheless!

ATONEMENT

at ZAC EFRON's beach house

TRUSSARDI-branded soaps

FORTUNE FEIMSTER as SARAH HUCKABEE SANDERS

A multi-hyphenate

CAPULET bromance

an intimate club w/ requisite gang-signs

i detect your silence

you you practised

personification of ALLURE

fresh face pummelled red & teal

according to that distant sheepdog narcissa

saliva syrupy like PEET'S coffee

FENDI sable coat hurriedly hung

stashed under the stairs

america's premier soft boi

the lab where he was born

SOLO SLUMBER PARTY

i luv honest emails that just begin 'hell:'

the road to hell is paved w/ too much cornbread

also good intentions

the road to hell is paved w/ good intentions

like u against a gate

or tennis grill (ur perfect teeth)

male bonding no longer in vogue

raccoon-dogs

make up ur dam mind

hopes up we branch out dutifully

cute boys like to be told they are smart

smart boys like to be told they are cute

cute smart boys like to be told nothing

but the markets!

ORIENTAL CENTO WITH LINES FROM O'HARA

Yellowing into an orient's lapse of life
the sun gallops, the ginkgo tree is suddenly cautious
In his drafty palace, there lived a statue
the single mouth howling
its simple moonlike pain
A trumpet bursts into night
nightingales slit each other's throats
the ominous silence of lust
'Is he blond and has he blue eyes?'
Evil and blue-green
no fainting pearl so delicate
to pluck you your eyes or flowers
'Be glad he'd gone before you got too upset'
as snow comes to the hushed ear
like a pontoon of silk
each crane is hot in the clouds, the steaming sky
We are beginning everything and forgetting freshly
the analogous excitements of his breath, our death
Pussywillows! oh you're still here
'Will you dance with me?'

———

By order of appearance:

[untitled]; The Air and Sex of Early Day; Augustus; Poem; A Romantic Poet to His Muse; [untitled]; To the Meadow; [untitled]; It's the Blue; Sonnet; A Classical Last Act; [untitled]; F#

EPHRATA, PENNSYLVANIA

Drunk girls catcall from a balcony

They say *smile*

& u do

U say *jump*

& they

HUSBANDS DO NOT BE ALARMED

Judith Butler describes heterosexuality as a rehearsed imitation of itself

~~I don't know if I hate reading~~

I hate reading

~~Ur stuck in my craw~~

Stick me in ur craw

~~Precise Powerade the same jackrabbit~~

Ur turnkey ur move-in ready

~~U don't have to touch it to know~~

I have all the time in the world

~~Move in baby one step closer to ur minivan~~

Now for my beaver costume

~~Wut will u soap first~~

ORIENTAL POEM BINGO

orange / mango / peach	smoke / ash / moon	rock / pebble / stone (fruit)
bone / body / wound	burn / singe / flame / heat	bury / swallow / alone
the seasons	ancestor / neighbour / border	*immediate relatives*
★	★	★
name / language / home	pronunciation / dialect	animal / beast / strength
mouth / teeth / tongue	mercy / memory / violence	rage / anger / fear / shame
soft / tender / kind	meaning / (american) dream	town / village / country
★	★	★
rice / bowl / ink	sauce / salt / skin / salivate	fish / egg / tomato / broth
river / ocean / sea / water	boat / train / airplane	cloud / sky / rain
break / bite / cut / sever	bug / blossom / bloom	song / silence / refusal
★	★	★
sweet / quiet / rot	grief / loss / exhaustion	fat / swollen / meat / milk
exotic / empty / eye	shadow / night / light / snow	land / mud / soil
comfort / document / witness	worship / hunger / devour	throat / belly / breath
★	★	★

DRINK BEFORE THE WAR

Lyft two blocks, Philadelphia native Lil Uzi, ur booty Chasm Ali

White chicks w/ digestive issues, exciting adventures at the nerd prom

No lobster tank, dignity sized for my purse

Given enough time, I could come up w/ something compelling

Michael from Mountains

Miss my own bed, punchline that never lands

A molehill, perhaps

Canadian navigator in upcycled cashmere

He's no better off, she can't hold a candle to me

Pop star w/ nose of golden retriever

New title: SENIOR ADVISOR for BEAUTY

The only kintsugi I know is ass crack

The detective in Japan who's a literal butt

U Aries u thick skull * MEAT *

Make luv like country mouse, I cherish ur prized drizzle

Palm me, nod encouragingly

Gimme osculations, a Ho-Ho-Kus

I am so fond of u

挪威森林 NORWEGIAN WOOD

i m bug, u r zapper, indiscriminate

i m trial judge, u r gang enhancement, disproportionate

ur new dude so swole looks infected

so toothy needs two brushes

stink rising, public nuisance, actually

u think i've moved on to some other toy, good stinky

pat my instrument, levi johnston was my sexual awakening

slice u open, chlorophyll exposed

hide in plain sight, beast bee shaffer

put down the wawa milk

lose favour, discounts cannot be combined

we may be a match but my taste has no equal

i say i luv u, no, i don't think so

it's not my fault i've always hated my face

the tyranny of ur good looks, in the classroom w/ the little desks

turning away from me, smiling like u just learned how

DINNER PARTY

Turnout so yuge the biggest I've ever seen

Boris Becker is bankrupt

Like Aria I've never been to Afghanistan

The shock of ur pale legs such that I'm weeping

That was a long shower

Ebi mean shrimp

Niall Horan my favourite One Directioner

Horrifically maimed as East End vigilante

He fit in my pocket

Like pre-fame Robert Pattinson

Maybe I'll go down to the Seaport before our hijinks

Meet cute in the swingiest of districts

Remake *Point Break* starring Jonathan Taylor Thomas

& born-again Christian Julian Casablancas

Tiresome as bathhouse w/ no exit

I don't think this president could stare straight into the eclipse

U hide rabbit in sweater, scratch & sniff wallpaper

Tell them u just have feral smell

Looking over my poems I impress myself

They go down so smooth

Unlike the pruno ur used to

Sorry I said wut is wrong w/ u

I meant wut is ur problem

PENGUIN BEACH

Was thinking it'd be embarrassing if Wayne didn't know me

(Embarrassing for Wayne)

What if ur mother, like former Senate Majority Leader Harry Reid,
hangs up the phone before ur done speaking ???

Ur impoverished taste

An unsolicited disclosure

Do not jump, will be stuck brushing elevator cock

Str8 boys, fingers discoloured, bonding over buffalo wings

The lean Shanghainese's frequent toilet trips arousing suspicion

Tonsil-hockey w/ stretched-out Keith Haring, toes curling like kung
pao shrimp

I wanted them to have a baby, chick cries over reputed celebrity break-up

A real dog can always tell a fake bitch

Trump says N-word is 'nu-clear'

Long hose visible when Blake adjusts himself

She's deeply moved by Louise Glück's C-word poem

He breaks up w/ her while Sade plays in the background

Turns down invite to Mubarak's seaside estate for rendezvous w/
boys on train

(Such majestic waves)

Boys awakened & affectionate, excitable as beagles

Ur not so tough after all

原来你是这种人 SO THAT'S HOW U R

male w/ patchy facial hair complimenting my sunglasses in havana

my impulses when talking to u r: (1) stroke u … (2) talk abt my poems

imagining u in crop top

target boys applauding rather than expressing uncontrollable disgust

snoopy balloons floating down fifth

i m thirsty for ur innocuous droplets

the dew on ur glabrous chest

highly desirable taste of anus

peach melba & potential insemination

most poems just verbs + body parts

i m v sensitive abt slit

你让我疯狂

u make me go mad!

when i receive u

ur wearing ur best smile

captive to u

like inflight movie in economy minus

i just can't look away

TAKE ME BACK INTO THE TWILIGHT

I have a hideous personality so it's harder for me

I paint ur nails

U flex for me

Surprise myself conversationally

They look past my Quasimodo lewks

Her mob past catching up to her

Too much dip on her chip, as it were

Mxn will really write poems abt their own parents having sex

U know wut my problem is ???

I'm too emotionally intelligent

My signature scent called COMMITTEE OF THE HOLE

Ur nose ruined in act of sabotage

I'm a panda, a tool for diplomacy

w/o u my life is *Colorless Tsukuru*

Thought I saw u in the street but it was just two bags of trash

My other issue being

How enamoured I am w/ quivering darkness

holding out for a hero w/ a hung cock

ANOTHER DREAMLESS NIGHT

yes yes   ppl menacing me   to me u'll always be frayed chinos & 23

   gallant fallen idol   startled   [sheepish?]   stepping forward

slightly bemused to be held   i own postage stamps

            change pillowcases often

   lights dim   are the cameras on   u commit ritual killing

music's off   show's over   ditch ur stroke mag   a poor edit

        u may be ☺ but find urself < ? >

  a study in pipe   dong for disappearing love

don't talk to strangers ahh … 天马行空 good things coming our way

   prayer hands   hold the suspense   no time to waste

today i had brandy-soaked cake   saw a shirt i liked   (burberry)

   toy soldiers   some animus   the ghosts who haven't bust

i demand clean sheets   intellectuals to share a bed w/

   do we understand one another   do u remember the words

NATE GROWING UP

hey, u, first row, dylann roof haircut

pick a card, any card

i want unsweet sweet tea

too-big-to-fail as life goal

sonia sanchez taught me the best swears

the answers u need won't be found at home

take the skin off, fire up the riposte

these aren't the nuggets ur looking for

why does imessage underline 'str8' as if to emphasize ur soft folds &
    sweet opening

come see, but only inside the dumpling

self-sabotaging like fox & spartan boy

i'm not terribly focused on morals of the story

a very good predictor, i predicted almost everything

at least that's how i remember it, lying perfectly still

JOCKSTRAP

butt-dialed by rudy

UVA boi suk & fuk in fairway

on this darkest nite

maestro of multi-volta risking arrest

i make u pome

from the bottom of my black heart

i like u wilkes-barre much

give u attention like white girl missing

every day is azn month

fav thing done 2 me lykke li

u don't look like u speak chinese

they anticipate u donda 2

correct misimpression of chains [for luv]

stupid u just happened 2 me

ur mind the finest cesspool

inside this empty orchard

the familiar concern that drugs can kill

but they promise 2 luv me more

we want 2 find anything

anything at all

HERE WE GO FOREVER

cody who goes both ways

they say familiarity accelerates impact

in secret huddles

tender kid w/ the kind tan

poached pears

vanilla ice cream

who was wearing the flip-flops?

i'm illiterate b/c i didn't have a high-school boyfriend

she smiled when they asked but

it's hard to get by w/ that kind of sincerity

in the wet warm place

hand-hold ur thing iz a sandwich

free rein in the blast hole

the mary jo bang

HAPPY POEM FOR HAPPY PPL

face-to-face w/ live fox in deep woods—scurrying justin sampling
    MLK

marrying minor baldwin—*stand for something* taken to mean 'chase
    that pussy'

hegemony of lazy susan & sugar factory

nation of immigrants under watchful white gaze

in illinois chicago sniffing glue

contemplating mania like horned sorceress whose lips garner attention

make me creme i call u cole swensen

redemption arc of frog & toad : no stone unturned / no cum left behind

we do not store confidential or personal data in jockstrap

intimacy of bully masking predisposition for dance

rick-roll urself sun bear did u want me to touch u under the table

where as here pooh & buddy distrust writers who don't read

stumble upon bag of apricots & respectable mouth instrument

can't bring disgraceful stinky out in public to dinners &c

i hope the insides of her ears itch—money not an issue if ur rich

nice story but also kitty dukakis

line on creme as sincere query

faithful baez we arroz con pollo—secret sauce secretly delicious chock full of nutz & bursting w/ references

make publication together so original iz translated

u know the story better than i do

sucker we r coming for u

MISSISSIPPI

made him sad cuz i'm only into sad bois

they have to look gud & smell nice

but they r sad cuz i don't want them

staring daggers at me

wives cuckolded, perhaps by o'hara

bad at games except!! mind games

head games by foreigner, the portuguese shawn mendes

jacob elordi described as 'deep in the closet'

girls down at the bon-ton, getting frisky at boscov's

daisy dukes in berlin, liz taylor's face revised more than this poem

hunter's password totally unassuming

'normal' as the ends of loaves

or possibly the end times

lower ur mortadella into my bologna

i eat cheap & drink expensively

cry into ur wedding soup

i know it's hard to believe

i'd never sex him

might as well be my cousin

w/ those man hands

LIE DETECTOR

CAN U TELL ME MORE ABT URSELF? WOULD U RATHER BE TALL OR UGLY? CAN I LEARN MORE ABT UR BACKGROUND? R U AVAILABLE TO CHAT? WHERE R U LOCATED? WOULD U WEAR MY EYES? WAS I SADISTICALLY DUPED BY ONLINE KINDNESS? IS UR BODY AS WELCOMING AS NEW MATTRESS? IS COLE REALLY 6'10"? CAN HIS HEART HANDLE SEEING ME IN NEAR-NUDITY? WILL A GOOD TIME BE HAD BY ALL? WUT TIME IS IT GOING TO BE? R U FAMILIAR W/ THE WASHINGTON, D.C., RESTAURANT FORMERLY KNOWN AS WHITE TIGER? R U BOTHERED BY THE SMALL SCENTED PENIS AT THE BAR? DOES UR ACHE BLOOM LIKE APRIL BLOSSOM? R U RELATED TO ITALIAN-AMERICAN KILLER FOXY KNOXY EXCEPT U NOT FOXY? R DEAD MOVIE STARS PERMITTED MORE FRENCH TOAST THAN NORMIES? R UR POKES RESERVED FOR GHOSTS NAMED PARKER? R 'DEAR JOHN' LETTERS NOW CONSIDERED RACIALLY INSENSITIVE? WHY DO SORDID LOVE AFFAIRS ALWAYS BEGIN ON THE LOWER EAST SIDE? WUT IF RILKE REINCARNATED INTO NEWT GINGRICH? WUT IF I'M TOO OLD FOR ALLEN GINSBERG? IF COMMUNISM IS REAL, IS THERE ANY REAL VALUE IN BEING SANTA'S FAVOURITE? IF A POEM STARTS OUT WRONG, SHOULD U EVEN CONTINUE? WHERE R ALL THE SHIPS THAT NEVER SAILED? R THEY ON FIRE? WOULD U LIKE TO SEE MY UNTITLED PACKET OF PANDEMIC POEMS? WUT IF THESE SIGNS COMPEL ME TO LITTER? WHICH POETS COULD PASS AS MINOR COMIC-BOOK VILLAINS? WHY R MY EARLIEST MEMORIES BOUNCING ON THE KNEE OF FEMALE INDONESIAN PRESIDENT MEGAWATI SUKARNOPUTRI? WUT IF THE CHAMPION DOESN'T LIKE BEING CALLED 'FEATHERWEIGHT'?

WUT IF FRANCINE ISN'T CROSS-EYED OR THE TARGET OF SALACIOUS RUMOURS? WUT IF I ONLY NEED FEEDBACK FROM JANET? DON SHARE? NO THANK U

DON'T LET ME SPEND THE NITE WITH TEARS

shawn mendes	heartbroken by john mayer	turning off wifi to hear god more clearly
orville peck	speaking afrikaans	contesting dry-cleaning bill ('hoekom horns')
rae armantrout	denouncing star-ledger obit	endorsing nikki haley
komunyakaa	sitting down w. the mooch	admiring sharp edges of beautiful object
paging paul legault	unmatching u on hinge	as we solidly consume cousin's tongue
inventing safeword	penile butter/penis dressing	smooth stone/copper canyon
bois w. new musculature	reasoned explanation for panting n meat sweats	
jalapeno poppers n fat leg of mutton	richly kissing/stillness like gasping in spanish	
hands around throat	celebratory voice vibrations	mr peck's pecker
poet's job pretend to like u	the rest procrastination	take daniel to dinner
mindful of travel look	mask of fringe n bead	a real boy n all in between

thicc fluffy parts moist like muesli

chris christie of pancakes

i forget ur claims in allocution

display threshold

touch threshold

monica youn on speed-dial

how fast to the top

likeable thighs humming none of dat quinoa shit

lonelier than abalone trader in east tennessee

my race is land azn

when pride month hits n iz sucked off for 99th time

when we drive past cracker barrel

raising a hand to starving devil

my heart's content

BREAKING EVERY RULE FOR ME

By the time u read this I will have stopped caring

Nikola Tesla joined ISIS

She is ur type, I m ur preferred font

I transmit poem to such journals as *Rat Vomit Revue*

edited by Menachem Begin

His wife sent anthrax to CAConrad

I think that's when my work really took off

His wife also moonlighted as the D.C. Sniper

That mattered to me less

U party animal 'Americano'

Why do dogs lick their own asshole

b/c their partner is under IA investigation

for discharging a weapon inside Applebee's

I hear that gun violence has become a real issue

I CHECKED UR CELLPHONE

my mom found & threw away my box of ants

i was so close to having enough ants

i hate when GIRLS die

i support breast cancer

oh this not a safe space suddenly

does anyone think global warming is a good thing

i luv lady gaga. i think she's a really interesting artist

just seen a sponge bob show on the tv

why the yellow man don't leave the octopus alone

me & my friends would've killed E.T. w/ hammers

i can tell u that much

so u mean to tell me that a shrimp fried this rice

& a cis teen built this chapel

i can't do this anymore

i got jury duty

MANDELA EFFECT

woke up surrounded by empty topo bottles, thinking of incestuous
   folgers commercial

these cheese puffs so cheesy & aryan

why i never feel u thinking abt me, is my counter broken

thumb on the scale, r u lost in the sauce

is it bad time to put out my new pome 'ysl' thank u

the ayatollah coming down from albany

his poetry quality declining precipitously since he lost me

i m queer icon he is false idol

main compartment suitable for two iphone 15 pro maxes

poets overcomplicating (overcompensating???) w/ 'weeping' mason
   jars like omg no wonder ppl hate us

to keep powder dry i splurge at kohl's

to splurge at kohl's i achieve inbox zero

to achieve inbox zero i unfriend everyone

v tired nobody make news today

KING OF THE WORLD

on this day

ur brimming w/ confidence

as if after years of getting got

u finally got them back

as tho in some deserted house

u'd found

some secret sign

(daybreak)

(a damsel in distress)

(a simple song)

on this day

we go back to our old routine

COWLICKS

how i wish this poem were abt horseshoes & lucky charms

& jesus as my editor

quieting the dead, sending totems of fortune

isn't all light meant for attracting attention

the root causes of immigration

jason momoa & the ppl matthew broderick put in an institution

the execution of all things

a real problem when scheduling can't decide

what official to send to which shooting

i hate antiques cuz freshness fetish

& 'antique' usually means exclusionary / exploitative

but i do luv when magic-hands james praises my old-hollywood cut

like most members of the leisure class, i don't know much abt anything

no longer edgy, no more black mirror

i know chicken kiev & mxn named dimitri

the russian tea room, how sabisu mean service

i sabisu u in intervu, fan sabisu

can't white gaze directly at ur brilliance

u cute in purple

u cute in any colour

fun size

thought u were my caroline but ur just kevin federline

jenny ur barely alive

answer me

SAINT DES SAINTS

1.

Koala rough fur
V counterintuitive
Like tall guy w/ short c
Delicate as Russian prince

2.

Stay inside for real, this heat yesterday—[temporal construction
 Merrillesque]—RAILED me

3.

Marking ur first & only appearance in a poem, smiling & pubescent

4.

How stupid u gotta be to believe I'm from the Oranges, a blue-
 tongued chow

5.

Boys in hard hats
Go down to the worksite to see how Whitman felt, O'Hara's papaya

6.

Here we are, incongruous like yachts in Minnesota

7.

Reevaluate my life, put brunch on top, abandoned hot dog kissing
tip of slipper

8.

When u get to a certain point
U care abt these things

CIRCUIT CITY IS BURNING

Pls advise him of his rights in the Monongahela

I've been asleep in Rapunzel's tower for many years

Ur requests transparent & pitiful

I can't send a pic that would cross an ethical line

Sometimes I read pretty words & feel absolutely nothing

[most poems]

Other times I'm submitting & the little voice says 'don't u think
    that's a bit much'

& I say SHUT UP MOM

A white businessman once told me

'we can't have a mayor named CHEW-EE'

He prob called me from his landline

I'm elite but not out of touch

Bring in the beagle brigade

Unmask ur student

U can be good cop

Daz cute daz cute

U got a sister ??? haha

Do u like it here

COMMENCEMENT ADDRESS

admin calls me the opposition party

even the whitest thing (lacrosse) is stolen

my luv for u finite since the republican party left me

budget cuts: ok to feed animals

we whimper & press together

each morning my grandfather gives me one diamond

i transmit to highest bidder & sexiest cad

writing inaugural poem for the gey one

i believe u called her a pretzel

at dinner we filled out the proust questionnaire—for *trait most
appreciated in friends* i put 'entertainment value'

luv when white reviewers talk abt that song & are like THE ONE
WHERE THEY ARE IN PARIS

select bois can enjoy my boudoir of saucy vignettes & fastidious
rubbings

all the aquinos are dead

ur writ of habeas corpus is granted

we will reopen subic bay

u can bet ur torah on it

u have nice eyes like lemur

wut we in the biz call a channel-changing face

u use me as human shield

u make an exceptional hostage negotiator

MY SAD CAPTAINS

—tired of this navel-gazing

soft, loose images

can't-be-bothered affectation

monied aesthetics

a pinstriped jacket

some green apples

can't forget the flowers

it's boring

it's *perversely* anonymous

never find clever lines like:

he thought u were goldie hawn

much cuter than camponi

meanwhile

hats off to u

needling me as i polish my horns

pansy poetry

a languid vacation

rich & white

a folded newspaper

gold class ring

lemony potatoes & chenin blanc

a light, inoffensive shade

it's anonymous, 'anonymous' being
too weak a word

like anybody could have written that

america is the blue jay of countries

the nurses are a few years old

chest the texture of store-brand jerky

admiring u in the manner henri
cole stares at trees

dick irresponsibly big

a tiny fist

SAN ANTONIO

The District Attorney is

getting recalled. On the elite bus they tell you

'good evening.' My happy place is

your pantry. I would like to get

two swallow tattoos. The greenest mantis says

'give me head.' He fathers four children

in my throat. You break your arm so the boy you like

will sign your cast. My favourite architecture is

desert modern but I'm not sure what that is. The Salem witch trials

were brought about by economic anxiety. Are you happy

with your love life? Are you

really?

SWALLOW YOUR POISON

I see a str8 porn where the guy has a double chin I feel better abt myself when they finish they clean my haus I give them stipend they insert into fannypack I don't know how I'm still drunk off the cough syrup Halsey gave me but hey a pay phone's ringing

∞

I have never witnessed boys swimming in lake water amidst long shimmering grasses the tequila song for obvious reasons I would like to I'm so bad at this who can relate

∞

We must ensure the finality of judgments this orange chameleon I named after Reverdy

∞

I tell myself I fucked up with you but I know I didn't there were two deaths that night I will never forget your tiny mirrors you are so beautiful why do you need them your perfect thighs I hate them I resent beauty I fucked up I'm sorry just the same

∞

One year at a friend's birthday party an Elton John impersonator performed two boys forcibly kissed me all I got was a lousy T-shirt to keep me honest

∞

I want to be the little tool fancy restaurants use to get crumbs off the starched tablecloth you can be the whitest white an extravagance of assumptions the benefit of the doubt I want to be the bendy straw in the best root beer float you've ever had fizz a dark cherry those heart-shaped spoons by Alessi I want to be your pale blue-pink cloud pressed blue-pink blue-pink into infinity forever please

慢走不送 C U NEXT TUESDAY

date worked out, driving luke evans back into the closet

i will schedule a bilateral meeting w/ musical accompaniment by matmos

spicer luv landis, date movie *pianist* (it's unrequited)

i was raised by a family of religious cheerleaders

we host meet-&-greets at the great wall restaurant

i show up trashed & write beautiful poems abt the lockdown

ask the stone lions if stuff is halal, if my pen name should be welfare kween

to enter the pantheon of greats, the olive garden cuz mad mex has a wait

some poems have iconic wordplay & create tension that way

other poems have basic, pedestrian language & r more abt vibes

in any case, predictable white guy who luvs hip-hop

polish up on ur casting-couch etiquette

we must build more prisons to expand jailhouse literacy

skin flashing, the cabana boys rush to collect wayward umbrellas

to make it up to u i let u fuck me into a vegetable

save ur strength! don't show us who u really r!

WORLD'S LAST RECORD STORE

new recruits w/ the hollow cheeks & big white teeth

we follow them back to the shady hotel

after the swordfight

he gives them his blessing

a walk in the park, he sez

chicken & duck talk, he sez

heaven, the club, he sez

music swelling, we build the plane as it's taking off

top gun as america's cry for help

take ur shit to the leather spa

go hang w/ the GSA kids & their terrible hair

early-morning songs but u will never be glamour

like dream flowers pink is the navy blue of india

australia accepts the credentials of the princess of tonga

monstrous!

colonialism, that is!

FUZZY DICE

mom says she was worried abt u spending three nights away

u say *don't worry it was w/ three different men*

i know u wrote that poem 'on the notes app' 'at the airport' 'waiting
for a delayed flight'

u sexpot of gumbo

carny ugly as sin

biden → nikki haley voter

don't let anyone tell u i'm averse to danger

u look like hell

there's big trouble in little china

i cure her cancerous foot

i eat only the egg roll

imperceptibly run toward the rat

battling it atop a volcano

finally defeating it in hand-to-paw combat

i'm good for my smarts

it's true

fuck my brains out

never felt so free

FIRST WE KILL ALL THE ROLY-POLIES

u cute as 300 roly-polies

i let them enter the revolving door so i can leave when they aren't
    watching

since u asked: ur photo—not racist enough

i virgin today

never met anyone like u today

millions of deaths before men started washing their hands

swimming thru this pome

like uninvited houseguest

[iz racially motivated ???]

i install a vulva for him, a white spaniard like jane freilicher

firing my therapist b/c falling apart isn't the look we want

no, make it a care package w/ strawberry twizzlers

first we get past the gender & sexuality stuff

then we go back to shaming ppl for being boring

do u think abt me, i say

too much, u say

all the while my miracle child

is crying out for more

sometimes straight thru

is a way out too

BING CHILLING

Pale children respect elders (South Park w/ Chinese characteristics)

Human girl gets Azn nerd (John Hughes w/ Chinese characteristics)

Sleep same room as family of eight (Prom night w/ Chinese characteristics)

Hotpot steam on cold day (Papal conclave w/ Chinese characteristics)

Slick Willie & Tricky Dick walk into a bar (Joke w/ Chinese characteristics)

Fit snugly alongside mute re-educated shark (Censorship w/ Chinese characteristics)

Replica of Dutch palace & pissing mermaid (Colonialism w/ Chinese characteristics)

Attractive foreign sailors playing soccer (Sportsmanship w/ Chinese characteristics)

First stop: Chinatown noodle shop (Overseas travel w/ Chinese characteristics)

Reanimate dodo in gilded nest colosseum (Exceptionalism w/ Chinese characteristics)

Sole outstanding candidate (Democracy w/ Chinese characteristics)

Feed live chickens to tigers from coach bus (Press freedom w/ Chinese characteristics)

Build camps in Xinjiang—like Yellowstone! (Land management w/ Chinese characteristics)

One-China policy (History w/ Chinese characteristics)

One in each colour (Shopping w/ Chinese characteristics)

Seven-day workweek (Self-care w/ Chinese characteristics)

Bitter melon juice I drink myself (Loneliness w/ Chinese characteristics)

ELEPHANT CASTLE

Some poets, ahem, Lorca: 'DERELICTE! Look at the homeless these vagrants']]

Vanessa Hudgens may actually be the Most Powerful Person in Hollywood]]

Kygo upstaging Whitney w/ Norwegian poontang]]

Ur salt stock taste like truck-nut gravy]]

Prayer my lunch order]]

Hillary Clinton false sniper fire]]

U not butter her bao w/ pork floss]]

Almost die recreating scene from chipmunk movie]]

Forché complimenting tooth necklace: 'I have something similar']]

Xie (泻, 'shay') also means diarrhea]]

Biden reads Hounds of Love into the Congressional Record]]

Vuong joins Danity Kane: pays off Stacey Abrams's card debt]]

Chink in the fence: blow out the candles]]

That emoji is water squirrel]]

Baby u feel so Deuteronomy]]

5* gutter-cleaning service]]

Ur gourd so extensive has anyone ever told u that See's Candies©]]

Tattoo boi find joy in my deprivation]]

Make me groan under weight of conquest]]

My mattress soft & my mind a playground]]

Depleted sacs & contraband lager]]

U: lush-cheeked & lovely]]

Me: profoundly preoccupied]]

RETURN TO SENDER

Truthfully I admire skinny legs like—

you

know. Unfed

Mark Doty didn't like ur Baked Alaska

I'm imagining those—

again

I'm not above such thoughts

趁热打铁

Strike while the iron's hot!—

That may be true but are men the cause of ur timidity

of emotion

The only inheritance that interests me is

cash money or real property

The only Double Ds being

direct deposit

Magnolias scenting my world

I go where I can

do the most damage

GENEALOGY

snip snip the well-fed flowers

support language artists / content creators

father a slice of pizza

date dressed as tequila sunrise

hi young boy stuffing girl on aeroplane

don't forget ur adult diaper

they admire ur laboured wealth creation ['wuz ur nationality']

too tall to be a sidekick

u must be the main squeeze

how much u reread my letter

ur wife a swedish fish

ur leetle butthole gone a long time

close the gates / lower the shutters

i need to have u for hours & hours

MOMOFUKU

I saw a movie of a little person

Or a little movie of a person

& micropenis named Rocco

Self-centred RBG

Flecks of sperm on her ~best~ ~dress~

It made her stepbrother cum

The one I want isn't around right now

All the good ones are emotionally unavailable

Fuck G-d!!

When the death panels reconvene I have some names

U & those rockfish lips

Simmer down pls

My number?? Write it on ur tits!!

There

PRETTY BOY EW

From New York to Texas

poets say some ppl go to bed

& never wake up

U know how many peons had to suffer for that

Amalfi Coast

flash-in-the-pan high

on some expensive skunk

How much fish u eat there

chasing ur lost relevance

w/ well-honed, time-honoured tactics

Crocodile Dundee

at Davos as guest of Good Housekeeping

& Eric batting his lashes at me

Can u believe I've never once mentioned human hair

that isn't, u know, attached to a human boy

Fistful of hair, u've been wanting it ever since

But I cannot give it to u

Fearless America First warrior

A whiff of desperation

No, anything but the cure

PRIVATE / PUBLIC

we patter excitedly on abt gus van sant

jibber-jabber abt how good maggie looks in that bodysuit

shining brilliantly then doused in green flames

w/ u i know feast & famine, probably in equal parts

repulse bay & passports up-to-date

we're impatient abt something

wanting to push the hair outta ur eyes

exchanging looks deep as tortilla

fast-forward to the part where we sleep together

whenever ur in a hurry to leave, throwing up a peace sign

i tell myself ur off to masturbate

despite all evidence to the contrary

say 'n' & mean nicholas, ur bum knee

carry ur skeleton but don't catch ur name

—guide me   —i'll bring him home in a box!

ANGEL'S SHARE

U were in my dream once, driving a little clown car

I could tell from ur sandals that u were Jesus

A v good lyricist that we also know as extremely kinky

U were diminished till dead

In my family the heart goes first so I make sure to stock up

Three for $5 or some such

Always show up on time, sneak cake under bridges

Thomas Crown Affair as indictment of late-stage capitalism

They have never been fisted by a deerskin glove

or tasked with changing all the pronouns on somebody's Wikipedia

In that underfunded planetarium, rickety & New Jersey

A dumb light show of desire

We invented it

Everyone had gone

I had a sensitive head

MOTHER OF MUSES

Look at u, so smug abt ur comfortable crack

Doctor's faxed over ur results: still a fantastic asshole

Something on ur chin, chopsticks in the air

Table manners missing like my gas money

No thank u, I need that like I need a lock in a sock: immediately

Ur w/ her now, fitness lady, the one u said had a splash of the coffee

Ur mould growing in somebody else's basement! finally!

I know u still swoon over packages naughty & nice

Milk-shits & boys who read

Oh! dasher, dancer, love handles out of reach

There u are, serving lines as petit fours

More stale than the Commonwealth of Nations

Not sure if it's worse to ignore u or listen to ur smart mouth

If the walls have ears they must be bleeding

Show hole

So small & grieving

WE'RE ONLY MOUTH

U green-eyed monster

w/ savage appraising eye

Generalissimo of cockblock

Chiang Kai-shek of blue balls

Subterfuge

U scab

U least-requested smoothie

U look like a seam slowly coming undone

I don't want to be part of this evil garden

I know I've stared rather indulgently

Like Kermit I held myself too open

That Sephora u terrorized will never recover

I'll make him guilelessly receptive

I'll make him screwy-eyed & lost w/in himself

I'll make him leap up to fetch another potato

The impotent king was thinking of pig's feet

glistening in its own juices

bronze & full of purpose

DO I REALLY HAVE NOTHING AT ALL

some boys chase success on lilypads

other boys lasso w/ strong pelvis

the 3 a.m. call nobody answers

doofy w/ bearing of eunuch

obsequious, emotionally suffused

always plotting

shunned like teen mom

i don't find angels terrifying

i enjoy them enigmatic & tight

i don't mean to be aleatory

pls be gussied up to see me

u may look forward to the excavation

survival is overrated

i wanna thrive

MOLLY RINGWALD / PORTRAIT OF A LADY

u were talking abt foreclosures

& then we kissed

i told a fan 'i agree, i am a great poet'

& u nodded dutifully

political spouse silda wall spitzer

stood by my side

the aircraft was snug & fit six ppl

they did not deliver on their promises

he drew a gun & fired

striking a seagull

she barricaded her brother in the closet

soothed u like wounded warrior

death by chocolate

it was grace

SECONDHAND GOD

wut u do on weekends, bluebook ???

every time i see u

i'm surprised by how good-looking u r

at best misleading

at worst inconclusive

eric's candied asshole

laid out for me like tatami

we went alone

eyes rolled back

whites showing like a furby's

pointed out the sights

pulled a thigh muscle

nothing but the sky falling

full of abandon

READY FOR THE ECSTASY

They say *I luv Youn* but u mishear & think they said 'I luv u.'

I luv places where they bring the iced tea & the cubes are made of tea.

It amazes me how golden opportunities stare ppl in the face & they just can't see it.

South Park Mickey sounds more Mickey than the real deal.

The ppl who most care abt titles are the least deserving of them.

I have been seen as a little radioactive.

The vibe is Hardy Boys meets Gorbachev.

Brought to u by Mindy Kaling's white daddy.

U say *I need financiers / not shopkeepers.*

She sez maybe ur feelings don't matter.

Ppl are too skeptical / too suspicious of others these days.

It does seem weird that he's in Venezia.

He sidles up to Eurotrash wearing fake D&G.

Is this wut Rilke meant by 'terrifying luv.'

The carpaccio is copacetic.

'Coriaceous' means having the texture of leather.

Face is harder to get right than body.

Look like moose & Tarantino had a baby.

Cut in half.

The boy's cock out.

The girl auditions for elegance.

Twenty mins to the Valley.

Such is my time posing as founder of the popular blog *Thrifty Boy*.

The thing abt journeys is some ppl never get there.

ALL THE HUSKIES ARE EATEN

one day aliens will discover my poems & ask *who is zac efron* do agnostics recognize one another or is it like chinese great crew lasting impact for once in my life the only apples i wanna see in a poem r adam's apples if conservatives r supposedly the only ones who luv this country why r their book titles always so doom & gloom where is their optimism i came to poetry even tho my family was not really literary they introduce me music of neopets when i was around 1.5 years that has characterized my relationship to language ever since i realize i could fold it in half & it would still be bigger than ur ambition but i was never into that willy-nilly like irina shayk bearding for bradley cooper really unfulfilled they stare blankly they r all boys the defending champ holding u almost satisfied on a dish

FORMER MUSE

DON'T WORRY, HE CAN'T HURT U NOW

(MY MESSAGE TO SIRHAN SIRHAN)

WE HAD BREAKFAST

BESIDES

NOBODY REALLY LIKES ME

BUT DON'T LET MY EX-MANAGER OFF THE HOOK

GRILL HER ABT THE $300K PAYMENT

HOW THE FUCK IS IT ALREADY 11:30

OH IT'S 11:03

I WAS LOOKING AT MY PHONE UPSIDE DOWN

I DON'T REMEMBER MUCH ABT THAT DAY

—I SEE THAT NOW

IT'S NOT A SAD THING

Walking into the fire

I don't want to

His name is Adam

He has a very nice thumb

The things that matter come in threes

Like bulls colliding w/ a gate

I won't bore u w/ the details

I want to forget them

Solitude or mortality

Or possibly living together

Ask Doogie Howser

Why u even have a phone

if u won't text me back

Someone like me

Someone holy

who still has dreams

COPY & PASTE

that pt in the evening/ /drinks start spilling/ /jw's sexy sketches/ /the other jw's chicken w salsa verde/ /i prefer poems that are verse-top/ / most of the time

struggling to find icarus/ /not sure if he ends up/ /dead or/ /available for vow renewals

still debating the merits of/ /masturbation/ /a groupon vacation/ /uninspired cheese of 'notes' section/ /*[breathily]*/ /ur so good at that

like alexa i'm always listening/ /i listen for open doors/ /u understand/ / the silence then

THINGS A BRIGHT BOY CAN DO

very fine degrees of meaning & shading   which are there   if u look
for them & absorb them

how wuz ur department store wench   i'm around later if u wanna
write for strangers

put that pussy to work   u can have wuteva u like   bob ur head along
to girls who make quesadillas

chiselled merchants trading stories   one, of coz, forgetful   telling
half-truths   in fits & starts

u say i'm the kind of bitch who gets run over   pls enlighten us   pls
explain wut u mean by that

maybe i'd say the same abt u   albeit softly   yes   i think i would

SOME FREE ADVICE

Sylvia *spider-men* so Swifty could *spider-boy*

U must believe in love as clickbait

Put the sweater on this time

Look at them & look at u

Shill for frottage

Gobs & gobs of cash

If I were an angel

I would be an angel w. hobbies

Do angels have a union / bargaining unit

Nice-assed foxes curled in my bed

Pitbull ft Ke$ha ('Timber')

We were here first

I drink from ur miracle-dick

Everything is the poor man's Pizza Hut

I am poor in character

Move ur hand

Light a candle for me

Those are the rules of the game

AREN'T YOU SUNSET?

Forgive me. I was a schemer —Czesław Miłosz

- the planets i set aside, for u, no doubt

    - taunting me, ur penn-station brunch

- all cream sweater & college degree, nearly fucked to death

    - like a race, cat got ur tongue, politically speaking

- boy, bear, balloon

    - double take, smile big, cozy indeed

- the love i felt, we need this one, alive

ACKNOWLEDGEMENTS

- This book is for Eric Issenberg

- Gratitude to:

Everyone at Coach House Books, especially Alana Wilcox, Crystal Sikma, & Nasser Hussain

Florian Krewer / Michael Werner Gallery, for the cover art

- Thank you to the editors of these journals for their fine taste:

air/light, Annulet, The Brooklyn Rail, The Brooklyn Review, Bullshit Lit, The Capilano Review, Cobra Milk, Dryland (now *Sin Cesar*), *Gayletter, Gigantic Sequins, Jet Fuel Review, The Malahat Review, Meniscus, North Dakota Quarterly, The Puritan* (now *The Ex-Puritan*), *The Recluse, Rougarou, Salt Hill Journal, Sonora Review, StorySouth, Subnivean, Superstition Review, TIMBER, Tyger Quarterly, Verse Daily, Yemassee* (now *Cola Literary Review*)

- Thanks, also, to my blurbers & readers, for their continued enthusiasm

MICHAEL CHANG (they/them) is the author of many volumes of poetry, including *Synthetic Jungle* (Northwestern University Press, 2023), *Toy Soldiers* (Action, Spectacle, 2024), and *Heroes* (Temz Review/845 Press, 2025). Their work has appeared in such publications as *AGNI*, the *American Poetry Review*, the *Harvard Review*, the *Iowa Review,* and *POETRY*. In Canada, their poems have appeared in the *Capilano Review*, *Contemporary Verse 2* (*CV2*), the *Ex-Puritan*, the *Malahat Review*, *PRISM International*, and elsewhere. They live in Manhattan.

Typeset in Aragon, PingFang, and Neutraface.

Printed at the Coach House on bpNichol Lane in Toronto, Ontario, on Zephyr Antique Laid paper, which was manufactured, acid-free, in Saint-Jérôme, Quebec, from second-growth forests. This book was printed with vegetable-based ink on a 1973 Heidelberg KORD offset litho press. Its pages were folded on a Baumfolder, gathered by hand, bound on a Sulby Auto-Minabinda, and trimmed on a Polar single-knife cutter.

Coach House is located in Toronto, which is on the traditional territory of many nations, including the Mississaugas of the Credit, the Anishnabeg, the Chippewa, the Haudenosaunee, and the Wendat peoples, and is now home to many diverse First Nations, Inuit, and Métis peoples. We acknowledge that Toronto is covered by Treaty 13 with the Mississaugas of the Credit. We are grateful to live and work on this land.

Cover art 'ride or fly I' by Florian Krewer, 2021, Oil on linen, 118 ½ × 94 ½ inches, 301 × 240 cm, Centre Pompidou, Paris, MNAM-CCI, © The Artist, courtesy Michael Werner Gallery
Cover and interior design by Crystal Sikma
Author photo by Christopher Fenimore

Coach House Books
80 bpNichol Lane
Toronto ON M5S 3J4
Canada

mail@chbooks.com
www.chbooks.com